Good Morning Miss Polly
Sharing Happiness

written by
Lynn C. Skinner

illustrated by
Ingrid Dohm

Good Morning Miss Polly
Copyright © 2022 by Lynn C. Skinner. All rights reserved.

No part of this publication may be reproduced, stored in a retrieval system or transmitted in any way by any means, electronic, mechanical, photocopy, recording or otherwise without the prior permission of the author except as provided by USA copyright law.

Published by Lynn C. Skinner
PO Box 34 | Alley, Georgia 30410 USA
Cover and Layout Design by Christina Hicks Creative

Published in the United States of America
Softcover 978-1-7336531-6-9
Ebook 978-1-7336531-7-6

This book belongs to:

_____

My thanks to many friends who shared Miss Polly stories with me.

Thanks also to the illustrator who turned the stories into beautiful artwork in watercolors.

Miss Polly was a remarkable lady. Although she was married and should have been known as Mrs. Polly, everyone just called her Miss Polly.

Even though Miss Polly was advanced in years, she always wore high heel shoes and long, dangling earrings which touched her shoulders.

Miss Polly's family was scattered and she was alone...

Decisions – decisions.

What was she to do? Then she had an idea!

She decided to volunteer at the local hospital. She could show kindness to the patients. She did this for many years.

Flowers brought joy and a smile to Miss Polly's face. She cared for the plants on her porch everyday.

Miss Polly began to miss a friend at a nursing home. Visiting the friend gave her another idea. She would go to the nursing home every Sunday afternoon and cheer the residents. Miss Polly always wore a smile.

Writing letters was an enjoyable activity for Miss Polly. As she remembered friends in other places, she began writing to them. Every day she wrote letters. She wrote long letters when she had time. Occasionally she just wrote a short note. Often the letter contained a funny picture which she drew or a cartoon she found.

Painting was a special hobby Miss Polly enjoyed. She illustrated several books.

One day Miss Polly decided to volunteer at the special needs high school class at the local school. Since she enjoyed art, she could produce art projects for the students. As she began to learn the unique interests of the students, she planned specific projects for each one.

One day she would offer large objects from cardboard which a student could color. Another day she had the students decorate the room with special paper chains. Oh, Miss Polly had so much fun thinking of projects the students would enjoy.

The neighborhood children loved Miss Polly. They knew that she welcomed them with joy, wisdom and maybe a lollipop or a cool drink of water on a hot day! She even enjoyed pushing baby Ford in his stroller.

Miss Polly was very generous with her time, her energy and her ideas. Because of her willingness to share, she received many awards and pictures. She was featured in the newspaper many times for her positive attitude and her ability to share happiness with everyone she met. These included the young, the old, the rich, the poor, her neighbors, the friends who lived many miles from her, the sick and those who were well.

Happiness often grows in our hearts when we think of others.

What about you? Have you shared any happiness today?

About the Author

Working with an individual on a regular basis teaches us so much. This story revolves around an amazing person as she adjusted to her many trials in a changing and challenging life. She constantly thought of others and put those thoughts into action. May we all be inspired everyday to follow Miss Polly's example.

About the Illustrator

Happiness is a choice. Whether your life is sunny or gloomy, find your smile by adjusting to life's situations. I trust that these illustrations will radiate my joy in art and the life of Miss Polly.

www.ingramcontent.com/pod-product-compliance
Lightning Source LLC
Chambersburg PA
CBHW042318090526
44583CB00024BA/3112